10-2-19
$ 15,30

Your Future as a
CHEF

HIGH-DEMAND CAREERS™

Your Future as a
CHEF

RACHEL GIVEN-WILSON AND SUSAN MEYER

Rosen
YA™

New York

Published in 2020 by The Rosen Publishing Group, Inc.
29 East 21st Street, New York, NY 10010

Library of Congress Cataloging-in-Publication Data

Names: Given-Wilson, Rachel, author. | Meyer, Susan, 1986– author.
Title: Your future as a chef / Rachel Given-Wilson and Susan Meyer.
Description: New York : Rosen Publishing, 2020. | Series: High-
demand careers | Includes bibliographical references and index.
Identifiers: LCCN 2018046826| ISBN 9781508187776
(library bound) | ISBN 9781508187769 (pbk.)
Subjects: LCSH: Cooking.
Classification: LCC TX714 .G583 2020 | DDC 641.3—dc23
LC record available at https://lccn.loc.gov/2018046826

Manufactured in China

Contents

The career of a chef can be wonderful for those who enjoy taking care and precision to create a delicious meal. From preparing the vegetables to creating the perfect flavor for the sauce to cooking the meat to the desired texture, cooking a good meal is something that many people take pleasure in. If you're someone who enjoys finding new ways to combine ingredients and create delicious flavors, the career of a chef might be perfect for you.

The chef's profession is a highly popular career choice among young people. This may be due, in part

Most chefs choose to pursue this career because they love cooking and get pleasure out of combining interesting or unusual ingredients and flavors.

to the number of celebrity chefs who can be seen living glamorous, globe-trotting lifestyles in the public eye. The reality of being a chef is, of course, not that glamorous. Being a chef is a tiring job that often involves long hours spent standing in a crowded and hot kitchen in a high-pressure environment. However, for those who are truly cut out for it, it can be extremely rewarding.

There are a wealth of different employment options available in the culinary industry. Chefs and cooks can be found in restaurants, cruise ships, and hotels, as well as private homes and even grocery stores. Most restaurant chefs begin as apprentices or commis and work their way up through the kitchen ranks. Some end up managing the kitchen as head chefs, while others decide to go independent and become private chefs. Learning more about these career choices can help you focus on which opportunities best suit your individual goals and interests.

Many aspiring chefs dream of opening their own restaurant one day. The restaurant industry is highly competitive, and it's important to have a strong vision and be prepared to work hard if you want to open your own restaurant. Melissa Scott and C. J. Jones are the co-owners of the lively soul food restaurant Soul Bar at Pals in Atlanta, Georgia. In a 2018 interview with RestaurantHER, they talked about their inspiration for the restaurant and their journey as entrepreneurs.

Scott cites her mother as her inspiration for entering the culinary world. "She taught me the balance of seasonings and how good food should taste…. She would make traditional dishes as well as mix in new innovative ingredients." The culinary duo decided to open their own restaurant because they had always wanted their own place to host events. "We wanted a place where we could create our own vibe…. It took us almost a year to find it and another year to rehab the space to our standards." The restaurant and bar opened in November 2015 and immediately became a popular dining spot. Scott and

Jones's success has taught them that "with hard work, perseverance, and faithfulness, anyone can have a vision in their mind, realize their dreams, and reach their goals, no matter how impossible it seems to others."

If you're interested in pursuing a career as a chef, it's helpful to learn about the different options that are out there for working in the culinary industry. Even if you're still in high school, there are steps you can take now to hone your culinary skills and start working toward your future as a chef!

Chapter 1

WHAT DOES IT TAKE TO BE A CHEF?

*I*f you're someone who loves food and cooking, you may be interested in pursuing a career as a chef. Many chefs and cooks develop their interest in the culinary industry from a young age, by helping out their parents or grandparents in the kitchen at home or figuring out how to combine different ingredients to produce new flavors themselves.

Being a professional chef can be an incredibly rewarding profession, but it it's also a lot of hard work. Many chefs work long hours, including nights, weekends, and holidays. While other people are out enjoying themselves at restaurants, chefs are stuck behind the scenes, making sure the food is up to par. It can also be a physically demanding job, with lots of time spent standing up in a hot and crowded kitchen. Therefore, it's important that aspiring chefs have a sincere passion for food preparation and cooking.

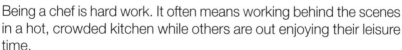

Being a chef is hard work. It often means working behind the scenes in a hot, crowded kitchen while others are out enjoying their leisure time.

For those considering a career as a chef, the future looks promising. According to 2018 data from the Bureau of Labor Statistics, the number of jobs for chefs and head cooks was projected to increase by 10 percent between 2016 and 2026. This is faster than the average job growth rate for all occupations. There are lots of exciting opportunities out there for specializing in different areas of cooking and food preparation.

THE INGREDIENTS FOR A SUCCESSFUL CHEF

There are a number of qualities that you should have if you want to be a chef. You must be creative and have a passion for food. Most people who set their sights on this career do it out of a love for creating new and unique flavor combinations in food. You must also have a willingness to learn—either in a culinary school or training program or on the job in a kitchen. There are an incredible number of skills that a chef has to learn, and the only way to develop these skills and techniques is to practice. A lot of learning to be a chef is simply doing something so many times that it becomes second nature.

Knife skills, for example, are an important part of being a chef. If you've ever seen professional chefs chopping vegetables, you can't help but be impressed by how quickly their hands move and how the pieces they chop are somehow perfectly uniform despite the great knife speed. This skill comes from hours and hours of practice (and more than a few bandages in the early stages).

Another important quality of any aspiring chef is to simply enjoy the act of food preparation in and of itself, as its own end rather than a means to an end. If you're hoping to achieve fame and fortune, you probably should not enter the culinary industry. Very few chefs in the industry get their own show on television or open restaurants in big cities all over the world. For every Emeril Lagasse, Anthony Bourdain, Rachael Ray, or Gordon Ramsay, there are many hundreds of men and women working anonymously all over the country in the kitchens of greasy spoon diners, big name chain eateries, mall food courts, and hotel restaurants. Good chefs appreciate food preparation and enjoy providing an essential service to people regardless of where they do it.

A good chef must also be creative. This, in part, means that the chef can think outside the box and make new, unique food combinations. To stand out in the culinary industry, chefs need to be able to think of ways to set their food apart from others and really forge an identity for themselves. A good chef must also be able to work well on a team. The head chef must be good at delegating responsibilities to the other chefs in the kitchen. The lower chefs must be able to take orders well and carry them out efficiently. Working as a chef is definitely not a good career path for people who like to work and succeed by themselves. The successes or failures of a kitchen on any given night depend upon the whole team.

A chef must work well under pressure. The atmosphere in a kitchen can range from a tense calm to a frenzied excitement. A chef cannot be fazed by people yelling orders, tight deadlines, and kitchen mishaps. Every second a chef spends in a kitchen involves a tight deadline. Only a few seconds separate an item that is undercooked from one that is just right or from one that is burned. Good chefs are always on their toes and display enormous grace under pressure.

Beyond all the strong mental qualities a chef must possess, there are some important physical ones, too. Training to be a chef can be like boot camp. Chefs are on their feet all night, and not just standing still. They are running back and forth from various burners to counters to the pantry to get more ingredients. There is also the enormous arm strength required to carry out tasks like chopping 40 pounds (18 kilograms) of potatoes or whisking egg whites into a meringue or deboning twelve ducks. Working in a kitchen isn't always a picnic, and it requires a lot of mental and physical strength, but to those who can take the heat, it can also be a lot of fun.

IS CULINARY SCHOOL THE RIGHT CHOICE?

If you wanted to be a biologist, you would most certainly have to go to school to study in a classroom, do research in the library and labs, and participate in field projects to gain the body of knowledge and practical skills necessary for a career in the field. But is the same true of cooking? In culinary school, you will learn some of the history and methods behind culinary arts, but most of what you will be doing is hands-on experiential learning. Is it better to learn in

Knowing how to use a knife safely and professionally is not something you learn overnight. Most chefs attend culinary school to obtain those skills.

a classroom setting than in a working kitchen in a real restaurant?

Some of the advantages of culinary school are that you are able to learn new skills in a controlled environment. You can also learn both local and global techniques. If you are working at a restaurant in a small Midwestern town hundreds of miles from the nearest big city, you might not have the same access to the increasingly popular and in-demand techniques of Malaysian cuisine, for example, or South American taste traditions. Formal academic training will give you a much broader range of knowledge, skills, techniques, and culinary references. You will also have hands-on, supportive, personalized help and be working with teachers whose primary goal is to mold you into a better chef.

Another advantage of formal training is that it is often part of a college or university program that allows students to work toward official certification as a chef. Upon graduation, when you are looking for your first job, you will already be recognized as a chef. This might help you start a few rungs up on the ladder. Not only will you possibly be able to start in a higher position in the kitchen, but you might also be eligible for a higher starting salary. Additionally, going to culinary school can help you make valuable connections in the restaurant world. You will get a well-rounded sense of culinary history and learn a number of different techniques and traditions.

There are some downsides to culinary school, however. Although there are shorter (and less prestigious) culinary training programs you can join, most degree-granting programs require two to four years of study in order to earn certification. Additionally, the cost of culinary school is much higher than other methods of training. Unlike

At culinary school, aspiring chefs spend years learning from experts and getting plenty of hands-on experience in the kitchen.

receiving your culinary training on the job, you are not getting paid when you attend culinary school. In fact, you are paying—often quite handsomely—to enroll in the classes. When you graduate from culinary school, you will still have to pay your dues in the kitchen. While culinary school might give you the knowledge, techniques, experience, and certification to start a little higher in the kitchen hierarchy and rise a little faster, it still takes a lot of hard work, long hours, and low wages to become a high-ranking chef.

Getting into a top culinary school can be incredibly competitive. There are far more people interested in attending the best schools than there are available places in the programs. You also have to be careful when choosing a school. Not all schools are created equal. Make sure to do your research and learn what sort of credentials the school will offer you and if it is well-known and respected in the culinary world. Try to find information on how many of the program's graduates get placed in culinary jobs soon after graduation and if the school boasts any alumni who have become prominent professionals in the field.

SOME SCHOOLS TO CONSIDER

If you decide that culinary school is the right choice for you, there are still a number of decisions to make. There are several questions you have to ask yourself to help choose a program that will be a good fit. Are you interested in attending—and can you afford—a two- or a four-year program? What is your budget for attending a culinary program? Do you want to go full-time or part-time? During the day or in the evening? What type of cooking are you interested in focusing on or specializing in?

What Will You Learn in Culinary School?

These sample questions, taken from Oklahoma Department of Career and Technology Information's 2016 Study Guide for Culinary Arts, provide a taste of the kind of knowledge you will need to get a job as a chef.

What type of oven contains fans that circulate air and distribute heat rapidly?
- a. convection (correct answer)
- b. multifunctional
- c. convention
- d. microwave

In a busy sandwich station, each ingredient must be:
- a. counted and weighed (correct answer)
- b. counted but not weighed
- c. weighed but not counted
- d. recalled only when needed

What is the purpose of an Intermezzo salad?
- a. palate cleanser (correct answer)
- b. dessert dish
- c. colon cleanser
- d. main course

There are a great number of culinary schools out there with good reputations that you can attend. There is an option to suit any aspiring chef's schedule, budget, and needs. There are four-year degree programs that offer bachelor's degrees and other nondegree courses that offer certificates that might take only a few months. The downside of this great variety of options is that it can be hard to choose just one.

One of the best-known culinary programs in the United States is the Culinary Institute of America (or, CIA, as it is sometimes called). This four-year university is the oldest culinary school in the United States. It was founded in 1946 in Connecticut. Today, however, it is located in Hyde Park, New York. The CIA is a residential school, meaning students live on campus while learning all about the world of culinary arts.

The CIA is a well-respected program both in the United States and around the world. It offers a well-rounded program that covers everything from American and international cooking techniques to nutrition science and sanitation, as well as hospitality and restaurant management. The goal of the institution is to produce well-rounded chefs ready for their first job in any kitchen. During the program, students have the opportunity to work in one of four on-campus restaurants and also to complete a one-semester externship. An externship is like an internship but is usually shorter in duration and is often set up by an institution. It is a period of time spent working in a restaurant for the purpose of gaining practical experience. An externship, like an internship, can be paid or unpaid.

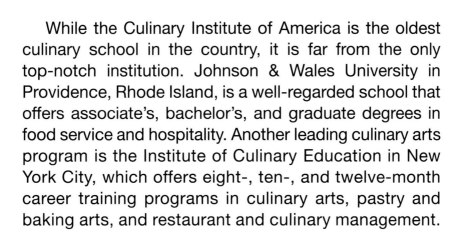

Some culinary schools offer specialty courses in learning about specific culinary traditions or trends, such as the farm-to-table movement.

While the Culinary Institute of America is the oldest culinary school in the country, it is far from the only top-notch institution. Johnson & Wales University in Providence, Rhode Island, is a well-regarded school that offers associate's, bachelor's, and graduate degrees in food service and hospitality. Another leading culinary arts program is the Institute of Culinary Education in New York City, which offers eight-, ten-, and twelve-month career training programs in culinary arts, pastry and baking arts, and restaurant and culinary management.

It was founded by Peter Kump, a founding member of the James Beard Foundation, an organization devoted to culinary excellence. The International Culinary Center in New York City and Campbell, California, offers classical French culinary training in addition to specialized programs in pastry arts, sommelier training, and the farm-to-table movement. It also offers an Italian studies program that includes language courses as well as culinary training and a study abroad experience in Parma, Italy.

APPLYING TO CULINARY SCHOOL

Many of the top culinary programs are extremely competitive and are unable to admit all of the qualified applicants who apply. It is therefore important for potential applicants to learn how to make sure that their applications stand out from the pack.

Some schools require transcripts, letters of recommendation, an essay explaining why the applicant wishes to study culinary arts, and a résumé with the applicant's background in the food service industry. Not all culinary schools ask for a background in the food service industry as a prerequisite for application, but some do.

Make sure to do your research when looking for the culinary school that is the perfect fit for you. Visit their websites and read any brochures and literature they have available. Look at their courses and see if they cover a range of techniques and skills, particularly those that you are most interested in learning. It is also important to consider the cost of the program and if it is within your reach. Will you be able to work part- or full-time while studying, or will the program require all your time and attention? The answer to this question will determine how you budget for tuition costs and living expenses. Finally, consider what you will be taking away from any program: will you have a meaningful and valuable certificate from a recognized and reputable culinary institution? Does the program offer professional connections and employment assistance or job placement after graduation? Will it give you the opportunity to intern or work in restaurants while in school? Don't be afraid to ask a lot of questions when you go to visit schools. If you can't visit all the schools you're interested in, make sure to contact an admissions officer or academic adviser with any questions you have.

Chapter 2

RESTAURANT CHEFS

According to 2018 data from the Bureau of Labor Statistics, 53 percent of chefs work in restaurant. When you picture a team of chefs at work in a restaurant kitchen, you probably imagine a hectic scene, with all the chefs rushing to get dishes ready in time for all the customers. Working in a restaurant is certainly hard work. Most restaurant chefs work at least full-time hours, and many work more than forty hours a week, including early mornings, late nights, and weekends. They spend most of that time on their feet.

A crowded kitchen can be a dangerous place, with health hazards such as hot cooking surfaces, slippery floors, and knives around. As a result, chefs are particularly prone to work injuries. To reduce the chances of injury, they usually wear long sleeves and nonslip shoes to work.

 Being a chef usually means working in a fast-paced environment. Restaurant kitchens are generally hot and crowded, and chefs need to make sure the dishes are prepared right on time.

Many restaurant kitchens employ a whole hierarchy of chefs, from head chefs or executive chefs down to prep cooks. Each of these types of chef plays an important role in keeping a busy kitchen on track to deliver delicious food to the restaurant's customers.

TYPES OF CHEF

You will notice that a lot of the names for different positions in the culinary arts derive from the French. This is because a lot of these terms and titles originated in France in the nineteenth century, but today they are used in kitchens all over the world. The word "chef" actually comes from the French *chef de cuisine* which means "chief of the kitchen" in English. Today, the word "chef" has come to mean not just the head of the kitchen, but any culinary professional regardless of his or her rank. The title executive chef or head chef is used to identify the person who is truly the kitchen chief. The executive chef is the ultimate authority in the kitchen. This person decides what should be on the menu and how it should be prepared, right down to how it should appear on the plate. These chefs manage the kitchen staff and are also often in charge of the ordering and purchasing of inventory—deciding what foods to buy and whom to buy them from.

Working under the executive chef is the sous-chef. In fact, "sous-chef" literally means "under chief" in French. The sous-chef is the second-in-command in the kitchen. This person is responsible for carrying out the executive chef's orders and instructions. The sous-chef is also responsible for filling in for the executive chef when he or she is off duty. Sometimes the head chef is the owner of the restaurant. In these cases, the sous-chef might actually be in charge of running the kitchen, while the head chef is occupied with running the restaurant as a whole. Smaller restaurants may not have a sous-chef, but large restaurants may have more than one—a day sous-chef and a night sous-chef. The sous-chef, as the second most important person in the kitchen, usually gets to handle the most expensive ingredients that some of the lower chefs don't get to work with.

Although the job varies from restaurant to restaurant, a sous-chef's duties may also include ordering supplies, training new staff, and expediting during lunch or dinner service. In the chef world, expediting means helping to pace the meals so that they go out of the kitchen at the right time. It is often a difficult juggling act to make sure the food for each table goes out at the same time and at the optimum temperature.

Below the sous-chef are the chefs de parties, also known as the line cooks or station cooks. Each line cook is in charge of a certain station in the kitchen. Say you go to a nice restaurant and order a steak that comes with a side of green beans. You also order a salad to start. If it is a large restaurant, your meal may be made by several different cooks. One line cook might operate the grill to make sure your steak comes out perfectly, while another might be in charge of cooking vegetables, and yet another might plate your salad. Everyone in a kitchen has to work as a team to make sure every customer's order is prepared correctly and sent out at just the right temperature and the right time.

There are even more kinds of chefs under the umbrella of station cooks because the chef who works at each station has a different title. The person who cooked your steak? That's the grill chef. The creator of your green beans was likely the sauté chef (sometimes known by the French word *saucier*), who is in charge of all sautéed items and their sauces. The culinary professional who plated your salad? This person is known as the garde-manger. The garde-manger is in charge of preparing cold items from salads to cold appetizers. The garde-manger is often

Desserts are usually prepared by a pastry chef. Pastry chefs are just one of the many different kinds of chefs you can find in a restaurant, each with their own specific skills.

considered a starting position in the kitchen because there is less training required to prepare some of these foods. Nevertheless, the garde-manger is a vitally important part of the kitchen staff. After all, the foods from the garde-manger's station are often responsible for the diners' first impressions of the meal.

There is an equally important person who handles the meal's final impression. If you still have any room left after your steak and you choose to order a dessert, it would be prepared by the pastry chef.

Below the station cook is the commis. The commis is an assistant or apprentice to the station cook. This is an entry-level position. Commis chefs are able to learn valuable skills from the cook under whom they are working. They can gain valuable knife and food preparation skills while experiencing the fast pace and pressures of a real kitchen environment.

Similar to the commis, but not always thought of as an apprentice position, is the prep cook. In many ways prep cooks are the backbone of the kitchen. They do a lot of the more basic, humble, physically grueling but essential tasks, like chopping all the vegetables for the night or mincing all the garlic. The prep cook might even butcher some of the less expensive cuts of meat so that they will be ready when the more experienced chefs are ready to use them.

All of these positions are very important in the kitchen— be it in a fashionable city restaurant, in a suburban chain eatery, on a cruise ship, or in someone's private home. In order to join the kitchen hierarchy, a chef must learn the basic skills necessary. Additionally, chefs must refine their palettes and learn new flavors and combinations to which they haven't yet been exposed.

A DAY IN THE LIFE OF A HEAD CHEF

A chef's day is very long—especially for a head chef or restaurant owner. A chef at an average-sized restaurant might arrive at nine or ten in the morning to make sure the necessary produce, meats, and other foods were delivered overnight. If there are problems, the chef might have to call the restaurant's suppliers to complain.

Mid-morning, the chef might start preparing (or supervising the preparation of) sauces and desserts or any food items that require a long time to cook or prepare. Around 11:30, the restaurant will open for lunch and the chef will need to start cranking out dishes for the busy lunch rush, which usually lasts until 2:00. From 2:00 until 4:00, the head chef might have time to review stocks and see what the kitchen needs to order. At 4:00, he or she can go over the specials for the evening with the sous-chefs and the waitstaff.

Depending on the restaurant, the dinner rush can last anywhere from 6:00 to 10:00 or 11:00 at night.

On a typical day, many chefs start out by preparing items such as sauces, which can take a long time to prepare. These items are then ready before the dinner rush starts.

After the last meal is served and the last customer is seen happily out the door, the chef can supervise what needs to be done for the next day. Only then can he or she head home around midnight or later to get a few hours of sleep and begin the whole process again the next morning.

INTERNSHIPS, APPRENTICESHIPS, AND YOUR FIRST JOB

Although some chefs will begin by trying to find a paying job—any job—in the culinary industry, there are a number of options for internships and apprenticeships as well.

A Tough Job

The day-to-day work in a kitchen is physically grueling. Chefs deal with heavy pans and ingredients—from bags of flour to sacks of potatoes—and are on their feet for long periods of time. In addition to gaining big muscles, new chefs must also learn to grow a thick skin. They must have a strong and confident personality and learn to take criticism well. In the high-pressure environment of a professional kitchen, even the smallest mistakes are often met with harsh feedback. This isn't true of all kitchens, of course, but for those who don't take constructive criticism well, becoming a chef is not a great career choice. New chefs will make a lot of mistakes before they learn how to do everything right, and while they're learning they have to put up with a lot of critical feedback—sometimes being

Before cooking schools became a common training ground for new chefs, many contemporary American chefs started out working as apprentices in restaurants all over the United States.

An apprenticeship means not just learning by observing, but being taught and mentored by a master in the industry. Some of these opportunities offer credentials just like culinary school programs. This means that, even for those chefs who opted to forego culinary school, they will have official certification of the acquisition of required skills and experience that they can put on their résumés when they look for jobs. The reasons for choosing to apprentice rather than attend culinary school can vary. The investment of time and money might keep some chefs out of the classroom, while others might find learning through hands-on, real-world professional experience to be a better fit for them.

Apprenticeship has its roots in European tradition. French chefs, some as young as thirteen years old, would learn the ways of cooking from master chefs. This system has remained largely unchanged in Europe, but the American apprenticeship system is less developed. There are fewer restaurants in the United States that are willing to take on novice chefs and train them, and laws in this country restrict the age of apprentices and limit how much they can work without pay. However, the American Culinary Federation (ACF) runs a two- and three-year national apprenticeship training program for culinary students in the United States.

For those who don't want or are unable to land a coveted apprenticeship, the best way to really kickstart a culinary career is to land your first job. There's no substitute for the kind of hands-on education and experience you can get in a kitchen. As you begin to look for a job, there are a number of things to consider. First of all, where would you like to work? Small town restaurants often have trouble finding good help, so there may be less competition for these positions. That said, the greatest concentration of restaurants, and particularly critically acclaimed restaurants, is usually in urban areas. If you do land a job at a top restaurant, don't expect a top-dollar salary to go with it. Because training under renowned chefs is considered a valuable learning experience, and because competition for these positions is so high, there is actually a good chance that the pay level is inversely proportional to the status of the restaurant.

Do you want to work in a large or small restaurant? A larger restaurant will have a larger staff and turn out a high number of dishes each night. However, a smaller restaurant, one with fewer chefs in the kitchen, may give you the opportunity of taking on greater and more varied responsibilities because there are so few "hands on deck." Working at

During an apprenticeship, a new chef gets to learn by working closely with an experienced chef. Many chefs start their careers this way.

a hotel can also provide a wide variety of restaurant and kitchen experiences. No matter where your first job is, you will learn a lot.

Given so many options, it can be difficult to choose where you want to work. A good rule of thumb is to simply look for jobs at the places that interest you most. If you want to be a pastry chef, you should look for jobs in pastry shops or restaurants where you could work under a strong pastry chef. If you want to work in a restaurant, you should look for the type of restaurant where you feel most comfortable and whose menu and cooking styles you most admire. Set your sights on a kitchen where you can get the best possible learning experience. Much like picking a culinary school, choosing a place to learn or continue learning will benefit your overall culinary education, even if it is not the highest-paying position.

Chapter 3

WORKING IN HOTELS, CAFETERIAS, DINERS, AND MORE

Although the classic image of a chef is in the huge kitchen of a restaurant, chefs can be found working in many other kinds of places as well. From hotels and cruise ships to school cafeterias, hospitals, and even grocery stores, chefs can be found preparing food behind the scenes. If you're thinking about becoming a chef, you should also think about finding the type of work environment that best suits your needs and personality.

WHERE DO CHEFS WORK?

Some chefs work in hotels and on cruise ships preparing food for the guests. A hotel offers a great variety of opportunities for a chef. Hotel kitchens are often very structured and very large because they are serving hundreds if not thousands of guests. When working in a hotel kitchen, a chef is not just preparing breakfast, lunch, and dinner, but also buffets, brunches, and room service, and catering for weddings, conferences, and other special events.

Chefs who specialize in off-site catering experience their own unique challenges. They might never know what the kitchen they will be working in will be like until they get there. They have to travel with all of their tools. Hardest of all, they have to serve a huge number of people all at once.

The food served in school cafeterias has improved greatly over the decades, as new emphasis has been placed on healthy options and fresh, quality ingredients. Cafeteria cooks work not only in schools, but also in colleges, office buildings, nursing homes, and hospitals all over the country. They have the difficult job of making mass amounts of food for a huge group of people. This food should be characterized not just by its quantity, but also by its quality. Cafeteria chefs may also have to follow stricter health and nutrition guidelines that will alter how their food will taste.

Another place that chefs may go unnoticed is in grocery stores. When people are doing their grocery shopping, they are usually thinking about all the food that they have to go home and cook themselves. But think about all the food in the store that's already prepared and cooked. If

Chefs who work in hotel kitchens have to prepare food for huge numbers of people on a regular basis. They often cater weddings and other events as well.

the grocery store has a salad bar, that means a prep cook had to chop and prepare all those vegetables, lettuces, and salads. If the deli counter has prepared pasta salads or preseasoned meats, a chef had to make those, too. And what grocery store would be complete without a bakery? A chef made those breads and desserts that are so hard to resist.

Food service workers who prepare food orders at fast-food restaurants, diners, and coffee shops are known as short-order cooks. This type of food takes a short time to prepare, hence the name! Short-order cooks prepare simple food such as sandwiches, burgers, and fries. They often prepare lots of orders at the same time.

MOVING UP THE RANKS IN THE KITCHEN

Culinary school is one option for obtaining a thorough knowledge of the culinary world. Even if you do go to culinary school, however, you cannot graduate and immediately become the head chef of your own restaurant. All chefs start at (or near) the bottom and work their way up through patience, perseverance, and practice. Ever wondered what Emeril Lagasse's first job in the food industry was? Emeril—who is the author of several books, owns multiple restaurants, and had a long-running cooking show—started out washing pots and pans in a bakery. Dieter Schorner, who was named one of the top pastry chefs in the world by *Time* magazine, started out salting pretzels.

Clearly, there's no shame in paying your dues in the culinary world. The only way to grow and learn as a chef is to start small, get your foot in a kitchen door, and work

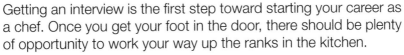
Getting an interview is the first step toward starting your career as a chef. Once you get your foot in the door, there should be plenty of opportunity to work your way up the ranks in the kitchen.

as hard as you can. First jobs are an important learning experience. One of the first things that every chef must learn is to be humble and to bring the same enthusiasm and attention to detail to any task, no matter how small or basic. From making sure each pretzel is expertly salted to mopping the floors of a fast-food restaurant, no chef should consider any job beneath him or her. Each job should be treated as a learning experience that will ultimately create a better, more well-rounded, and more talented and experienced chef.

One of the reasons that even culinary school graduates must apprentice and practice their craft is that it's hard to understand what work is like in a professional kitchen until you've experienced it firsthand.

Top Five Cooking Shows

Some people think they know what it's like to be a chef because they've watched numerous cooking shows featuring professional chefs. Although these shows don't represent the reality of what it's like to be a chef, aspiring chefs can certainly pick up some tricks of the trade by watching these shows. Many of them serve up some pretty great entertainment as well.

The following are some of the most popular cooking shows on television:

1. *Hell's Kitchen.* In this Fox series based on the British series of the same name, celebrity chef Gordon Ramsay puts competing chefs through tough challenges in a high-pressure environment and then gives them brutally honest feedback. The winner gets to be head chef at a restaurant.

2. *The Next Iron Chef.* The Food Network's *The Next Iron Chef* is a spin-off of the original *Iron Chef America* and sends its contestants to compete against each other in exotic locations across the world. The winning chef from each season gets to compete on *Iron Chef America.*

In the TV show *Hell's Kitchen*, chefs compete against each other in a number of culinary challenges. The show is hosted by celebrity chef Gordon Ramsay.

(continued on the next page)

(continued from the previous page)

3. *Chopped.* **Hosted by Ted Allen of** *Queer Eye for the Straight Guy,* **this Food Network show pits chefs against each other as they cook a three-course meal. The challenge is that they have to include ingredients from a mystery box, which can include things like seaweed and Animal Crackers!**

4. *MasterChef.* **This Fox show features amateurs instead of professionals and has them competing to create dishes while facing challenges, such as including unusual ingredients.**

5. *Top Chef.* **The Bravo show** *Top Chef* **has been popular since it first aired in 2006. The show pits rising chefs against each other in a series of entertaining challenges that encourage them to show their culinary creativity. One challenge is Restaurant Wars, in which each team has to launch a pop-up restaurant and compete against each other.**

THE SWEET LIFE OF A PASTRY CHEF

Few people can't appreciate the sweet creations of a good pastry chef. In a typical restaurant, the pastry chef might be in charge of baking bread for the restaurant, as well as preparing the best part of any meal: the dessert. From ice cream and custard to tarts and cakes, these specially trained chefs know their way around sugar and flour.

Being a pastry chef is very different from being a regular line or station cook. The pastry chef typically works independently of the other chefs. This chef often starts the day very early and finishes his or her work by the lunch rush. It is also a different type of culinary work involving a number of unique and specialized skills and cooking and baking techniques. What makes most cooking both fun and challenging is that the chef must use a degree of instinct to season something just right. Pastry chefs can be improvisational and mix and measure ingredients "on the fly" and to taste. With baking and dessert making, however, the chef needs to demonstrate an attention to detail and concern for proper math and precise measurements. If the butter is not the proper temperature or the precise measurement of an ingredient is not added at exactly the right time, the whole dessert could be a disaster.

When it comes to desserts, there are usually two people involved: the pastry chef who produces the dessert and the service person who ultimately puts it on the plate. The service person is in charge of plating the dessert with the appropriate garnish and sauces and making it lovely ... just before you devour every last bite.

DEVELOPING GOOD WORK HABITS IN THE KITCHEN

Whether you are trailing (working for free at a restaurant as a sort of tryout), apprenticing, or working your first job, it is important to make a good impression. You want to arrive on time, if not early, for your shift every day. If you're not on time, you will look disorganized, which is one thing no chef can afford to be. When you have available time, you should also volunteer for any shifts that need filling, especially the weekend and holiday ones. It is important to make the best of on-the-job learning. Find a mentor who will help guide you and give you feedback. Feedback early in your career—both positive and negative—is important to any chef's growth and maturation as a culinary professional.

Equally important is learning to establish a daily plan that you can execute the same way every day. Take notes on each step that you are responsible for and make sure you keep your quality consistent no matter what step in the process you are handling. Good chefs always keep thorough notes, with a prep list and a diagram of what their workstation will look like. You might think you can

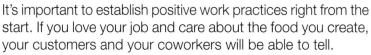

It's important to establish positive work practices right from the start. If you love your job and care about the food you create, your customers and your coworkers will be able to tell.

remember everything without writing things down, but keep in mind that the prep list and station diagram will be changing as the menu changes, so keeping notes is a good way to avoid getting confused or missing something.

You must master any task that is given to you. Developing good work habits and discipline early is the best thing you can do for yourself as a young chef. This way as you develop more skills and take on more responsibility, you have a good foundation to fall back on. Whether working in the kitchen of a restaurant, a hotel, or a cafeteria, every chef needs the same basic skills and the same qualities to succeed.

Chapter 4

PRIVATE CHEFS AND RESTAURANT OWNERS

For experienced chefs, there are a number of opportunities to branch out in the culinary industry. Some chefs choose to escape the chaos of a commercial kitchen to work as a private chef in somebody's household. Others may decide to open their own restaurants. These can be rewarding career paths to take, but they also come with their own challenges.

PRIVATE CHEFS

Some chefs don't prepare food for large crowds of people at restaurants or hotels, but instead cook for a small number of people. Personal chefs usually work in their employers' homes. They are completely in charge of the preparation of meals, usually even including choosing and buying the ingredients. They must plan a menu based on the preferences, dietary restrictions, and allergies of the family for whom they cook. This type of job can allow

Some chefs opt out of working in busy restaurants or hotel kitchens and instead work as private chefs, preparing food for families in their own homes.

personal chefs greater freedom and more time off than that enjoyed by restaurant chefs.

THE BUSINESS OF BEING A CHEF

Having a good business sense is a quality that is sometimes overlooked but one that chefs really need to be successful. This is particularly true if one of your goals is to own your own restaurant—whether it is a place of your own design or a franchise of a larger chain restaurant. However, even if you don't aspire to own a restaurant and are happy operating someone else's kitchen, it's still important to understand how and why a restaurant makes money. It's even more important to understand how and why a restaurant loses money.

A restaurant is, first and foremost, a type of business. The only way the business stays open is if it makes enough money to cover all its expenses, ideally with a healthy profit left over. In addition to knowing how

Many chefs dream of one day opening their own restaurant. The restaurant industry is highly competitive, so it's important to have a strong business plan before starting out.

to cook, a chef who wants to own a restaurant also must have financial and managerial skills. Just as you can go to school to learn how to cook and prepare food, you can also take classes in learning to run a small business. It is easy to educate yourself on how to run a restaurant, as long as you realize the magnitude of the undertaking.

Restaurants are notoriously hard businesses to keep open. There's a common myth that most restaurants fail in the first year. That's not entirely true. A study featured in *Forbes* magazine reported that only 17 percent of restaurants close in the first year. However, opening and running a successful restaurant is not an easy thing to do. It helps if you have an original concept for your restaurant, rather than just another pizza place or another noodle place.

Restaurants fail for a number of different reasons. Many of these reasons have nothing to do with the quality of the food. While the food is the most important part of any restaurant, it is not

Few restaurants succeed because of the quality of the food alone. Popular restaurants attract repeat customers because they provide a pleasant dining experience.

the only part. A chef can make the best menu in the world and the restaurant can still fail if he or she doesn't take into account a multitude of other variables.

A Restaurant Run by Grandmas

You're never too old to become a chef. At least, that's one lesson you could take from the success of Enoteca Maria, a restaurant in Staten Island, New York, where the chefs are *nonnas*. (Nonna is the Italian word for grandmother). The owner, Jody Scaravella, was inspired to open the restaurant by his tight-knit Italian family and his gratitude to his grandmother Maria for preserving his family's cultural traditions. Out of a desire to preserve these Italian culinary traditions, he invited nonnas from different regions of Italy to cook at Enoteca Maria.

"I realized that my grandmother had been the repository of our family culture and identity. And I found out that, like her, millions of grandmothers all over the world pass down their heritage to their grandchildren," Scaravella wrote on the restaurant's website. "Moved by the wish of sharing Italian grandmothers' culinary culture, I opened a restaurant."

The concept was so successful that Enoteca Maria now invites grandmothers from other parts of the world to be guest cooks once a week. Customers who visit Enoteca Maria can now enjoy culinary delights made by grandmas from Turkey, Siberia, Poland, Russian, Brazil, and Colombia, as well as, of course, Italy. The success of Enoteca Maria goes to show that an original concept can take you a long way when it comes to opening a restaurant.

The restaurant must be in a highly visible location where people can get to it easily. A good staff must be assembled and maintained. The owner must hire waitstaff, hosts, and other front-of-house positions, as well as all of the assistant chef positions in the kitchen. The front of house positions are just as important as those in the kitchen because these people will interact with customers in a way that the chef and cooks can't. The restaurant-owning chef also has to consider the ambience of the restaurant. The overall feel of the restaurant should be inviting and should complement the food that the restaurant serves. You wouldn't want to order a $40 filet mignon in a place with sticky floors and plastic furniture. The look of the restaurant goes a long way to selling the food before it even gets to the plate.

WOMEN IN THE CULINARY INDUSTRY

Although women still do the majority of cooking in family homes, women make up only 19 percent of chefs and 7 percent of head chefs, according to 2018 statistics reported by ABC News. In 2018, the online food ordering company Grubhub launched a campaign called RestaurantHER, designed to raise awareness about this gender discrepancy in the restaurant industry and encourage people to support women-owned restaurants.

"Closing the gender gap that leaves women occupying fewer than 20 percent of chef positions in the US will ultimately introduce new creativity and expertise into our restaurants, and no doubt elevate the entire culinary industry," said Matt Maloney, Grubhub's CEO, in a press release.

Although the culinary industry has traditionally been dominated by men, more and more women are becoming chefs and restaurant owners.

The campaign's website features an interactive map showing people where their local women-owned restaurants are, as well as interviews with female restaurant owners. In one such interview, Courtney Cowen, the owner of Milk Jar Cookies, describes why she thinks it's important to support women-owned restaurants. "The positions of power, be it the restaurant owner or the manager, they are historically male [but] it's definitely changing. It's very inspiring to go into a place and see that it's a female chef." Cowen says that running her own business is a dream come true. To aspiring young chefs, she says, "You really have to go for it and put your entire self into it."

Chapter 5

THE FUTURE OF THE CULINARY INDUSTRY

The future looks promising for aspiring chefs. According to 2018 data from the Bureau of Labor Statistics, income growth was projected to lead to increased demand for high-quality dishes and a wider variety of dining options during the decade leading up to 2026. More restaurants are likely to open as a result of this demand. Moreover, with more and more customers demanding fresh and healthy meals cooked from scratch, there is an additional demand for chefs to work at meal delivery companies such as Blue Apron, Plated, and Hello Fresh. In fact, according to a 2016 article on Upserve.com, there is a severe shortage in the number of qualified chefs in the country. So, if you're interested in working as a chef, now is a great time to be beginning your career!

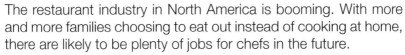

The restaurant industry in North America is booming. With more and more families choosing to eat out instead of cooking at home, there are likely to be plenty of jobs for chefs in the future.

THE CULINARY INDUSTRY AND THE ECONOMY

The job of a chef is central to the modern North American lifestyle. The culinary industry is continuously growing and expanding, as more and more people enjoy going out to eat or ordering takeout from a favorite neighborhood restaurant as opposed to going to the store, buying food, cooking, and cleaning up. In the 1950s, the restaurant industry accounted for only a quarter of the total dollars Americans spent on food. In 2017, money spent in restaurants accounted for almost half of that total dollar amount, according to the National Restaurant Association's 2017 State of the Industry report.

According to the same report, restaurant industry sales were around $799 billion a year, and restaurants employed more than fourteen million people in 2017. Chefs, waiters, dishwashers, managers, and restaurant workers accounted for around 10 percent of the US workforce. Restaurants are not just important for people who are looking to celebrate a special occasion, share leisure time with friends, or enjoy a delicious meal they didn't have to prepare themselves. Restaurants are an essential part of the economy itself.

While not all chef and food preparation jobs are recession proof, there is a great deal of growth in the restaurant industry. The Bureau of Labor Statistics projects that there will be around 14,100 new jobs created for chefs, cooks, and food preparation workers by 2026. If you enjoy food, cooking, and making people happy with your culinary creations, you could be one of them!

CULINARY TRENDS AND THE FUTURE OF FOOD

The trend for farm-to-table food is likely to have an impact on the future of the culinary industry, impacting chefs in the restaurant industry and beyond. Although the phrase "farm-to-table" has been around since the sixties, the farm-to-table movement has been gaining momentum since around 2010, with increasing numbers of restaurant goers demanding locally sourced, healthy food. Chefs of the future, especially those who plan to open their own restaurants, will need to have a deeper understanding of how to meet these needs.

The popularity of services such as Blue Apron, Plated, and Hello Fresh is leading to an increased demand for chefs. These services provide freshly prepared food delivered on a weekly or even daily basis, allowing customers to cook their own food easily from carefully portioned ingredients. Although the customers do their own cooking, this recipes needs to be created and tested

Services such as Blue Apron deliver freshly prepared ingredients for customers to cook at home. These recipes have been designed and tested by professional chefs.

by professional chefs. If these types of services continue to increase in popularity, there is likely to be an increase in the number of jobs available for trained chefs.

When Amazon purchased Whole Foods in 2017, many people began to wonder how the increased availability of fresh food delivery would impact the future of the culinary industry. In an interview with CNBC, Marcus Samuelsson, celebrity chef and owner of Red Rooster restaurant in Harlem, New York City, offered the following thoughts on some of the potential positive and negative outcomes of the trend toward online grocery shopping:

> Harlem is filled with small food entrepreneurs—Aaron the Jamaican guy I buy my juice from on 125th Street, Marc at the coffee shop on Lenox and 118th, Mustafa selling shea butter, the Senegalese lady selling food to construction workers on-site daily. It's these kinds of local places that give Harlem—or any New York neighborhood—its character and enhance the special qualities of city life. My regular interaction with these local businesses keeps me grounded and connected to the community. When on demand shopping dominates, what happens to the local mom-and-pop businesses, the bodegas, grocery stores, and delis?

On the other hand, Samuelsson believes that grocery shopping on demand could help to make fresh food affordable to more people. He suggests that technology can help small local businesses compete with online giants such as Amazon. "At this critical time of the consolidation and changing distribution network of our food system,

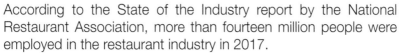According to the State of the Industry report by the National Restaurant Association, more than fourteen million people were employed in the restaurant industry in 2017.

we can envision (and build) a future where quality food is accessible to everyone at every income level."

GETTING YOUR FOOT IN THE KITCHEN DOOR

So how do you go about landing your first job? As with any job, the first step is to write your résumé. It's important to emphasize all academic, volunteer, internship, and work experience that could be applicable and demonstrate your love of and passion for food. This is especially true if you are a new chef who might not have a long list of direct restaurant experience to put down. Consider any experience that might be applicable. If you worked at a farmers' market selling produce or even on a farm, you can use this experience to demonstrate your familiarity with the farm-to-table ethic of modern cuisine. If you were a waiter or dishwasher in a restaurant previously, this can demonstrate your knowledge of how a kitchen works and your familiarity with restaurant hours. Even if you worked as a teller in a bank, the useful math skills you acquired might be relevant if you are an aspiring pastry chef who deals with math and measurements on a daily basis. These skills could also come in handy if you work in a smaller restaurant where you may be able to share responsibility for inventory management and balancing the books. Just remember, the most important thing about your résumé is that it conveys who you are, why you are passionate about food, and why you would be a good asset to any restaurant.

Make sure you do a lot of research on the restaurants to which you are applying. Study and memorize the menus, learn about the head chef, and read reviews. This is important both so that you will know if you want to apply there and also so that you can answer questions about why you want to work there if you get an interview. The interviewer will want to know why you chose their restaurant and what you are hoping to bring to the restaurant, as well as what you are hoping to take away from the experience. Successful chefs say that putting your résumé out there and waiting for interviews and job offers is an exercise in patience and persistence. It can

Preparing for Job Interviews

If you get an interview for a job as a chef, be prepared to answer a lot of questions about your interest in food and what inspires you. You might be asked where you've traveled and what flavors are your favorite. The interviewer will also likely be interested in your goals and where you would like to be in a few years. The point of the interview is both to see if you are a good fit for the restaurant and to see if the restaurant is a good fit for you. In the interview, as in your résumé, the best thing you can do is convey your passion for food and cooking. Don't worry as much about technical questions or knowing every possible cooking technique. Restaurants hiring new chefs are more concerned that you have the essential qualities and makings of a good chef, not necessarily every last skill. If you have the desire, will, passion, creativity, and basic talent required to be a chef, they will often be willing to train you on the job.

take a long time and require a lot of legwork. The important thing is not to give up.

Some restaurants ask applicants to "trail" in the restaurant before signing them on to work full-time. Trailing really just means working for free at the restaurant so the chefs can see how well you mesh with the rest of the team and with the restaurant as a whole. Because line chefs must work together like a well-oiled machine to get everything

No job is recession proof, but as long as people enjoy going out to restaurants to relax and enjoy time with friends and family, there will be jobs available for chefs.

done, it is very important that each new chef who is hired works well with the other chefs. Unpaid trailing might sound like a raw deal, but it's actually a great opportunity. While the restaurant is determining if the chef is right for it, the chef can also use this time to determine if the restaurant is the right choice for him or her. This gives potential chefs a chance to see how the kitchen operates and if they would prefer to work in a larger or smaller restaurant or one that serves a different style of food.

CHOOSING A CAREER AS A CHEF

Choosing to become a chef means choosing long hours and few weekends or holidays off, but for someone who has a passion for food, it can be an ideal path to a rewarding career. If you love cooking and delighting people with your culinary creations, a career as a chef could be perfect for you. This is one high-demand career that is here to stay!

Glossary

APPRENTICESHIP An arrangement in which someone learns a trade by working alongside an experienced professional in that trade.

CHEFS DE PARTIE A chef who works just below the sous-chef. Also known as a line cook or station cook.

COMMIS CHEF A position as an apprentice chef.

CULINARY Relating to food and cooking.

EXECUTIVE CHEF The chef who is in charge of running the kitchen; also known as the head chef.

FARM-TO-TABLE A social movement that encourages the consumption of locally produced food directly from the farmer or producer.

GARDE-MANGER The chef in charge of preparing cold items from salads to cold appetizers. Considered a starting position in a kitchen.

GARNISH A food item used to decorate a meal, rather than intended for eating.

HEAD CHEF The chef who is in charge of running the kitchen; also known as the executive chef.

LINE COOK A chef who is responsible for preparing ingredients and putting dishes together; also known as a station cook.

PASTRY CHEF A station cook who specializes in making desserts.

PREP COOK A cook who does the most basic food preparation work in the kitchen, such as chopping vegetables.

PREP LIST A list of each dish being prepared and the ingredients, utensils, and equipment needed to prepare it; made and used by chefs to organize their work and stay on track.

PRESEASONED Description of food that has already been seasoned.

SAUTÉ CHEF The chef who is in charge of all sautéed items and their sauces; sometimes known by the French word *saucier*.

SOMMELIER A person trained in the art of wine and wine pairing; also known as a wine steward.

SOUS-CHEF The chef who is second-in-command in the kitchen after the executive or head chef; from the French phrase meaning "under-chef."

STATION COOK A chef who is responsible for preparing ingredients and putting dishes together; also known as a line cook.

STATION DIAGRAM A diagram showing the layout of a station or work space in the kitchen; used by chefs to organize their work.

For More Information

American Culinary Federation
180 Center Place Way
St. Augustine, FL 32095
(904) 824-4468
Website: https://www.acfchefs.org
Facebook and Twitter: @ACFChefs
Instagram: @ACF_Chefs
The American Culinary Federation is a national
    membership organization for chefs and other
    culinary professionals, offering educational
    resources and events.

American Personal and Private Chef Association (APPCA)
4572 Delaware Street
San Diego, CA 92116
(800) 644-8389
Website: https://www.personalchef.com
Facebook: @personalchefassociation
APPCA offers training and educational programs
    through the American Personal and Private Chef
    Institute (APPCI).

Bureau of Labor Statistics
Postal Square Building, 2 Massachusetts Avenue NE
Washington, DC 20212
(202) 691-5200
Website: https://www.bls.gov/home.htm
Twitter: @BLS_gov
The Bureau of Labor Statistics provides comprehensive
    information and statistics about all types of labor,

including qualifications required for each profession and links to additional job information resources.

Canadian Association of Foodservice Professionals (CAFP)
130 – 10691 Shellbridge Way
Richmond, BC V6X 2W8
(604) 248-0215
Website: https://cafp.ca
Twitter: @WeAreCAFP
The Canadian Association of Foodservice Professionals is a national membership association providing networking and educational resources for culinary professionals.

Culinary Federation (CF)
Facebook and Instagram: @CulinaryFederation
Twitter: @CulinaryFed
The Culinary Federation is Canada's largest nonprofit organization serving professionals in the culinary industry. Its Canadian Culinary Institute offers certification for chefs.

National Restaurant Association
2055 L Street, Suite 700
Washington, DC 20036
(202) 331-5900
Website: https://www.restaurant.org/Home
Facebook and Twitter: @WeRRestaurants
The National Restaurant Association is an industry organization representing more than 380,000

restaurant locations. It offers advocacy, events, and educational resources.

United States Personal Chef Association (USPCA)
PO Box 56
Gotha, FL 34734
(800) 995-2138
Website: https://www.uspca.com
Facebook: @USPCAchefs
Instagram and Twitter: @USPCA
USPCA is a membership organization providing training, resources, and events to help personal chefs manage their businesses.

For Further Reading

America's Test Kitchen. *The Complete Cookbook for Young Chefs.* Naperville, IL: Sourcebooks Jabberwocky, 2018.

Bedell, J. M. *So You Want to Be a Chef? How to Get Started in the World of Culinary Arts.* New York, NY: Aladdin/Beyond Words, 2013.

Gay, Kathlyn. *Celebrity Chefs: Anne Burrell.* New York, NY: Enslow Publishing, 2016.

Harper, Charise Mericle, Aurelie Blard-Quintard, and Andrea Miller. *Next Best Junior Chef: Lights, Camera, Cook!* Boston, MA: Houghton Mifflin Harcourt, 2017.

Harper, Charise Mericle, Aurelie Blard-Quintard, and Andrea Miller. *Next Best Junior Chef 2: The Heat Is On.* Boston, MA: Houghton Mifflin Harcourt, 2017.

Mason, Helen. *Chef.* New York, NY: Gareth Stevens Publishing, 2015.

Rauf, Don. *Celebrity Chefs: Jamie Oliver.* New York, NY: Enslow Publishing, 2016.

Rauf, Don. *Celebrity Chefs: Rachael Ray.* New York, NY: Enslow Publishing, 2016.

Stern, Sam. *Cooking Up a Storm: The Teen Survival Cookbook.* London, UK: Walker Books, 2014.

Tomei, Annette, Tracey Biscontini, and Michele Thomas. *Culinary Careers for Dummies.* Hoboken, NJ: John Wiley and Sons, 2013.

Bibliography

American Culinary Federation. "About ACF." Retrieved September 20, 2018. https://www.acfchefs.org/ACF /About/ACF/About.

Anderson-Minshall, Diane. "Top 5 Reality Cooking Competitions." ThoughtCo, January 12, 2018. https://www.thoughtco.com/top-five-reality -cooking-competitions-2874462.

Bureau of Labor Statistics. "Chefs and Head Cooks." Retrieved September 20, 2018. https://www.bls.gov /ooh/food-preparation-and-serving/chefs-and-head -cooks.htm.

Culinary Federation. "About CF." Retrieved September 20, 2018. https://www.culinaryfederation.ca.

Culinary Schools.org. "Career Resources and Information for Chefs and Cooks." Retrieved September 20, 2018. https://www.culinaryschools .org/career-info/#context/api/listings/prefilter.

Doyle, Alison. "10 Cool Jobs in the Food Industry." The Balance Careers, October 29, 2018. https://www .thebalancecareers.com/cool-jobs-food -industry-2064051.

Enoteca Maria. "Our Story." Retrieved September 20, 2018. http://www.enotecamaria.com/wp/our-story.

Harrington, Hannah. "Take Your Cooks Back from Blue Apron." Upserve Restaurant Insider, August 9, 2016. https://upserve.com/restaurant-insider/take-your -cooks-back-from-blue-apron.

Lamb, Adam. "Where Do We Go from Here? The Future of Culinary Culture." Foodable Network, April 5, 2017. https://www.foodabletv.com/blog/2017/4/5 /the-future-of-food-and-culinary-culture.

National Restaurant Association. "State of the Industry 2017." Retrieved September 24, 2018. https://www .restaurant.org/News-Research/Research/soi.

Oklahoma Department of Career Technology and Information. "Culinary Arts Study Guide." 2016. https://www.okcareertech.org/educators /assessments-and-testing/testing/study-guides /study-guides-ok-works-2015-2016/CulinaryArtsSG .pdf.

Ozimek, Adam. "No, Most Restaurants Don't Fail in the First Year." *Forbes*, January 29, 2017. https://www .princetonreview.com/careers/32/chef.

Princeton Review. "Careers: Chef." Retrieved September 20, 2018. https://www.princetonreview .com/careers/32/chef.

Princeton Review. "A Day in the Life of a Chef." Retrieved September 20, 2018. https://www .princetonreview.com/careers/32/chef.

RestaurantHER. "About RestaurantHER." Retrieved September 20, 2018. https://restauranther.com /about.

RestaurantHER. "Courtney Cowan Puts Her All into Every Batch." Retrieved September 24, 2018. https://restauranther.com.

RestaurantHER. "A Q&A with Soul Bar at Pals in Atlanta." February 16, 2018. https://restauranther .com/q-and-a/soul-bar-at-pals.

Samuelsson, Marcus. "Amazon Whole Foods Deal: My Biggest Hopes and Fears." CNBC: Tech, July 11, 2017. https://www.cnbc.com/2017/07/11/amazons

-prime-responsibility-in-whole-foods-deal
-commentary.html.

Sijufy, Sarah. "Nonna is Making Dinner and All of New York Is Invited." Fodor's Travel, February 7, 2017. https://www.fodors.com/news/nonna-is-making -dinner-and-all-of-new-york-city-is-invited-12301.

Sorgule, Paul. "9 Reasons to Be a Chef." We Are Chefs, October 25, 2017. https://wearechefs .com/2017/10/25/be-something-special-be-a-chef.

Thrillist Food. "The 25 Most Influential TV Chefs of All Time, Ranked." Thrillist, February 6, 2018. https:// www.thrillist.com/eat/nation/best-tv-chefs-cooking -shows#.

Index

ABOUT THE AUTHORS

Rachel Given-Wilson has written and edited a number of nonfiction books for teenagers, including the Tech Girls series of books about careers for girls in STEM industries. She lives in Brooklyn with her family.

Susan Meyer is a writer living and working in New York City—one of the greatest food cities in the world. Meyer is an amateur chef operating within the severe limitations of her apartment's small kitchen, but she leaves the serious culinary creations up to the professionals.

PHOTO CREDITS

Cover, p. 63 Dragon Images/Shutterstock.com; pp. 6–7, interior pages (background) Volodymyr Goinyk/Shutterstock.com; p. 7 (inset) Jacob Lund/Shutterstock.com; p. 11 Boston Globe /Getty Images; pp. 14–15 Prostock-studio/Shutterstock.com; p. 17 Javier Larrea/age fotostock/Getty Images; p. 21 Jirayut Trista/Shutterstock.com; p. 25 Neville Elder/Corbis Historical /Getty Images; p. 28 Anna Pustynnikova/Shutterstock.com; pp. 30–31 Molpix/Shutterstock.com; pp. 34–35 Smith Collection/Iconica/Getty Images; p. 39 blackliz/Shutterstock.com; p. 41 Steve Debenport/E+/Getty Images; p. 43 PictureLux /The Hollywood Archive/Alamy Stock Photo; p. 46 Sergey Chumakov/Shutterstock.com; p. 49 Matthias Ritzmann /Corbis/Getty Images; pp. 50–51 Glenn van der Knijff /Lonely Planet Images/Getty Images; pp. 52–53 Wilfried Krecichwost/Photographer's Choice RF/Getty Images; pp. 56–57 Ian Spanier/Image Source/Getty Images; p. 59 Alex Wong/Getty Images; p. 61 Scott Eisen/Getty Images; pp. 66–67 Monkey Business Images/Shutterstock.com.

Design and Layout: Nicole Russo-Duca; Photo Researcher: Sherri Jackson